Plains Women

Women in the American West

Paula Bartley and

Cathy Loxton

CAMBRIDGE
UNIVERSITY PRESS

MW00659059

Published by the Press Syndicate of the University of Cambridge
The Pitt Building, Trumpington Street, Cambridge CB2 1RP
40 West 20th Street, New York, NY 10011–4211, USA
10 Stamford Road, Oakleigh, Victoria 3166, Australia

© Cambridge University Press 1991

First published 1991
Reprinted 1992

Printed in Great Britain at the University Press, Cambridge

British Library cataloguing-in-publication data

Bartley, Paula
Plains women: women in the American West.
1. United States. Western states. Women, history
I. Title II. Loxton, Cathy
305.40978

ISBN 0–521–38616–0

Library of Congress cataloging-in-publication data

Bartley, Paula
Plains women: women in the American West /
Paula Bartley and Cathy Loxton.
p. cm.—(Women in history series)
ISBN 0–521–38616–0
1. Women pioneers—West (U.S.)—History.
2. Women—West (U.S.)—History. 3. West (U.S.)—
History. I. Loxton, Cathy. II. Title. III. Series.
F596.B274 1991
978'.0082—dc20 90–33135
CIP

Author's note

We would like to thank all the following people for their help, advice and support: Helen Leigh, Carol Adams, Stephanie Boyd, Helen Crosby and the authors of the Women's West Teaching Guide.

Glossary

Words printed in *italic* in the text appear in the Glossary on page 47.

Notice to teachers

The contents of this book are in the copyright of Cambridge University Press. Unauthorised copying of any of the pages is illegal and also goes against the interests of the authors.

For authorised copying please check that your school has a licence (through the Local Education Authority) from the Copyright Licensing Agency which enables you to copy small parts of the text in limited numbers.

VN

Contents

Introduction

About this book

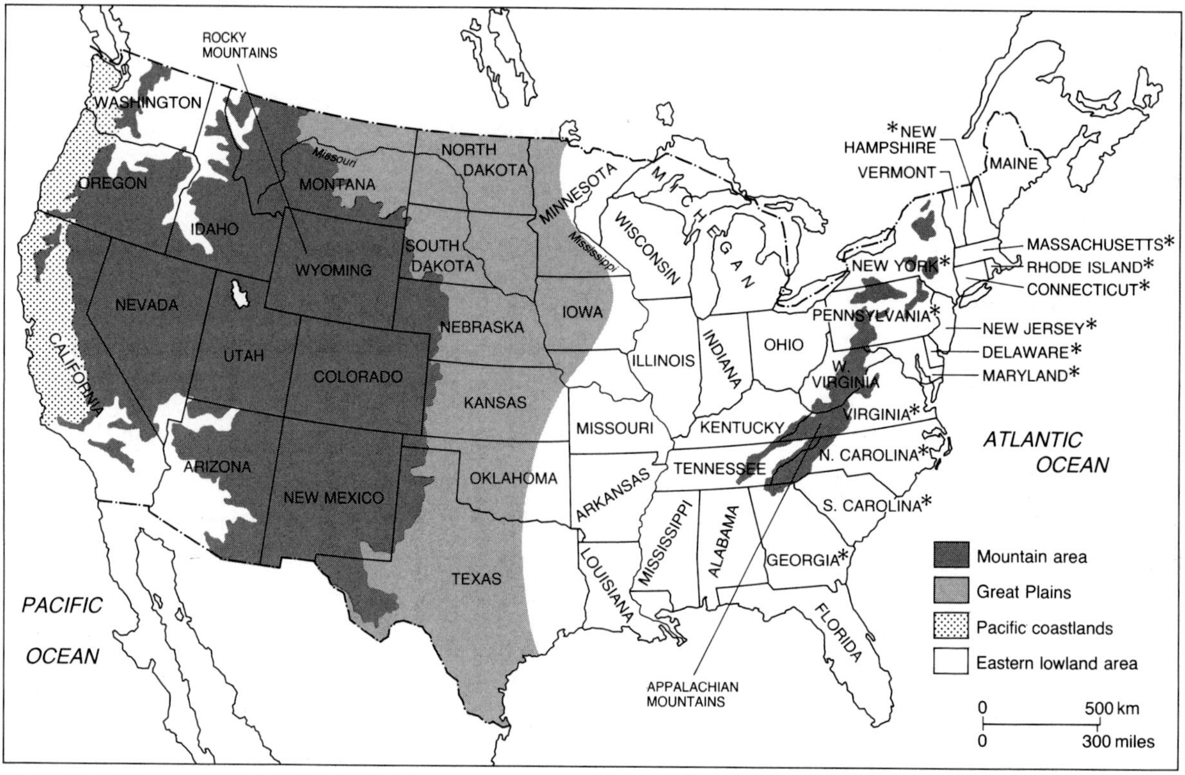

By 1912 there were 48 states in the United States of America. Those marked with an asterisk (*) are the original thirteen states. They were former British colonies and they won their independence in 1783.

Until recently, books on the American West have usually concentrated on the myth of how the West was won. It has been a violent myth which has emphasised adventure and fighting. Women have been virtually absent from the history of this American West. When they have appeared, they have tended to be in the person of the 'refined' lady of the school-ma'am or the 'bad' lady of the outlaw or the prostitute. Sometimes women were seen as the 'gentle tamers' of rough and rowdy men.

This book is about the daily lives of ordinary women, from both an Indian and white background, who lived and worked on the *Plains*. It tells of their travels, of how they coped in their everyday lives, of their problems and their successes.

Sources

It is not easy to find primary sources about women's lives. Most printed material focuses upon laws, battles and conflict, not upon daily events.

To uncover information about women's lives on the Plains it has been necessary to look at more private source materials such as diaries and letters. It is important to remember that these more personal accounts are written from one person's viewpoint. One woman's experience might not be the same as another's. So a wide variety of materials has to be read to gain a true picture of what life was like then.

Diaries

Diaries are an important source for understanding the lives of women pioneers. They contain eye-witness accounts which recall incidents which were still very fresh in the mind of the writer. As a record of what women felt at the time they are an invaluable source. Many women kept diaries which were read by others in the family. Some were even sent to their friends and relations back home or to newspapers for publication.

Letters

Many women were separated from their families who were in the East of the United States, or Europe, so rather more letters than usual were written. These letters often give a good insight into the everyday life of homesteading and sometimes reflect a person's more private feelings.

Oral evidence

Oral evidence is very valuable for historians writing a record of the lives of ordinary people. These memories are a rich source of information and provide material that can never be found in official documents. People who lived through an event or remembered details about their daily lives have shared their memories with others, who have recorded or written down what they said.

The Indians did not write about their experiences as this was not part of their culture, so this type of evidence is very important in exploring their past. An Indian woman, called Pretty Shield, for example, talked about her life to a white man called Frank Linderman through an interpreter using sign language. 'I told Sign-talker the things that are in this book, and have signed the paper with my thumb.'

Oral evidence, however, presents many problems. Sometimes, many years after the event, people's memories might be distorted or faulty. In the case of Pretty Shield, many details recorded about her life might be wrong. See if you can find the weaknesses in this source!

Paintings

Paintings can show something about the time in which the painter lived. The main drawback is that the artist is free to paint what he or she wishes. So there may be very different interpretations of the same event. For instance, many artists concentrated on the more pleasant side of pioneer life.

Photographs

Pioneers often carried around photographs of loved ones. Especially popular were those taken as a memory of children who died at a young age. Most photographs were taken in a studio after the long overland journey and showed women and their families posing for their relatives and friends back home. Some white photographers took pictures of Indians to sell back East to people curious to learn about them.

Early cameras were slow and cumbersome. Everyone had to stand quite still for several seconds whilst the photographer was taking their picture. If someone moved, even slightly, the picture was blurred. Only a few photographs of life on the Plains show people in an unguarded moment.

Autobiographies

Autobiographies show us what people of the time felt and thought, but they must be treated with some caution. They often have weaknesses similar to those of oral history, as people's memories can be distorted over a period of many years. Another problem is that they may be written to please a certain audience.

1 Plains Indians

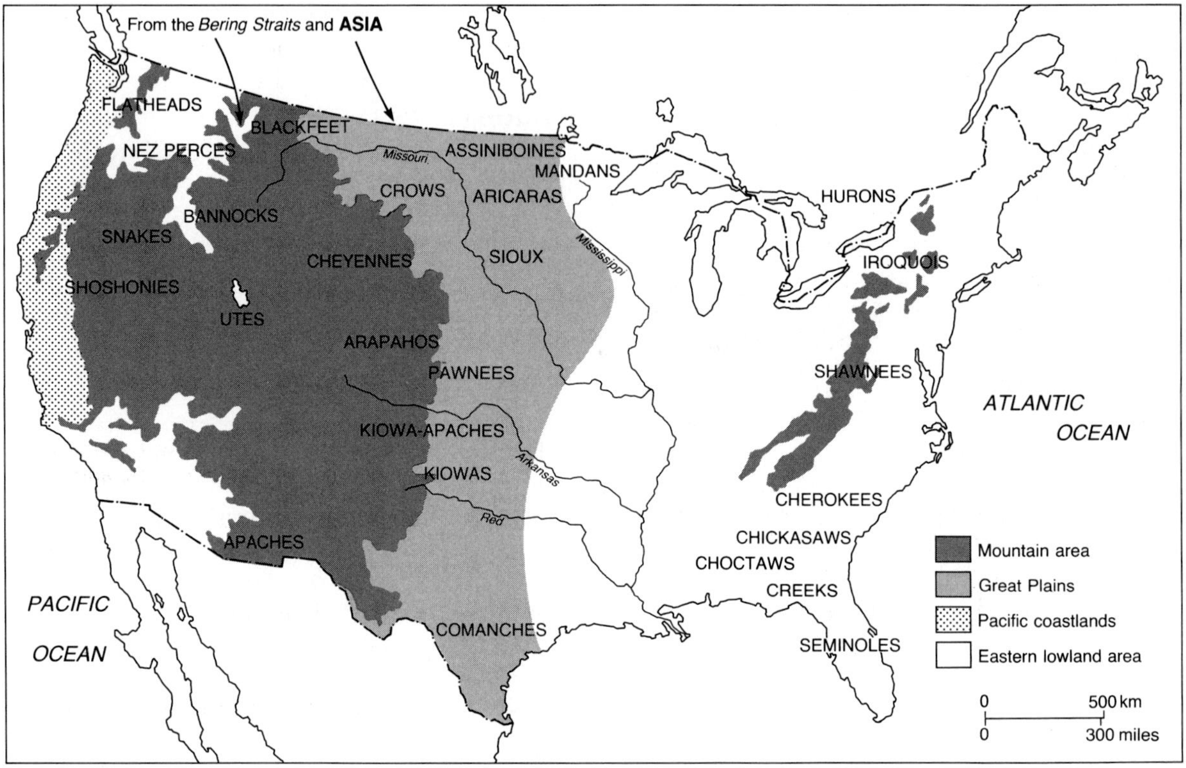

In the mid 19th century there were many Indian tribes living on and around the Plains

Indians lived in America centuries before the arrival of white or black people. When and from where the Plains Indians came we do not really know. Most historians and *anthropologists* believe that Indians travelled across the Bering Straits, from Asia, tens of thousands of years ago, long before the sea divided Asia from America. By the 19th century there were many different groups of Indians living on the Plains. The main groups were the Apache, Arapaho, Cheyenne, Comanche, Crow, Kiowa and the Sioux. All these groups spoke different languages, but shared a common culture and life-style based on the buffalo.

Buffalo

Buffalo roamed in large herds all over this wild, desolate prairie landscape. These great fierce animals were essential to the survival of the Plains Indians. Food, clothing, housing and other essentials were all obtained from the buffalo. Buffalo provided the Indians with meat, *tipi* covers, footwear, containers, shields, charms, paint from the blood and *gall*, thread from *sinew*, bone for tools and weapons, hair to braid into ropes, cleaned intestines for water carriers and cooking utensils. *Rawhide*, soaked in water, could be wrapped around broken

Indian women tanning hides

limbs; this rawhide would later harden into a splint as hard as plaster. Nothing of the buffalo was wasted.

The coming of the horse

Before the horse was brought into America by the Spanish in 1540, Indian men hunted the buffalo on foot. It was a physically demanding and dangerous job tracking down these ferocious beasts. With the arrival of the horse, life became easier. In the days before horse-back travel, Indians were limited in the amount of buffalo meat they could carry. With horses, men hunted much further afield, carrying back large quantities of meat for their group. Just one ordinary animal, the horse, transformed the lives of the Plains Indians, giving them more freedom and plentiful food.

Work

In many tribes the jobs of the men and the women were seen as being equally important. The men were the hunters and fighters, owning weapons, stallions and *geldings*. Women were farmers, housebuilders, tool-makers, weavers, artists and removal experts. In some tribes the women owned house equipment, game killed by the men, the dogs, mares and colts. Pretty Shield, a Crow Indian, describes women's work:

> War, killing meat, and bringing it into camp, horse-stealing, and taking care of horses, gave our men plenty of hard work, and they had to be in shape to fight at any time, day or night. We women had our children to care for, meat to cook, and to dry, robes to dress, skins to tan, clothes, *lodges* and *moccasins* to make. Besides these things we not only pitched the lodges, but took them down and packed the horses and the *travois*, when we moved camp, yes, and we gathered the wood for our fires too. We were busy, especially when we were going to move.
>
> *Frank Linderman, Pretty Shield, oral account, 1932*

Building the home

Indians on the Plains did not live a settled life in a cosy house but were constantly on the move. Buffalo did not stay in one place for long, so if the Indians wanted to eat, they had to follow the great herds of buffalo around the Plains. To make it quick and easy to travel, the Plains Indians lived in tipis. Tipis, made of buffalo hides, could be kept warm in winter and were, above all, simple to move. Although tipis varied in size, most were made of 18–20 buffalo hides sewn together. Women spent a long time working on the skins and getting them ready for use. It required much skill and patience to make a tipi. First of all the buffalo hides were *tanned*. Each hide was scraped clean of flesh and fat from the inside and hair from the outside. Brains, liver, *soapweed* and grease were mixed together and rubbed into both sides of the hide. Then the hide was folded up and the tanning mixture allowed to soak in overnight. In the morning the hide was put in the sun to dry. Once dry, the tanned skin was stretched on pegs to make the hide supple and soft. It took about ten days to tan a hide.

Making a tipi was a difficult task so women helped each other. Sisters, mothers and friends all took a hide home with them to tan.

This extract was written by Mr Grinnell who had watched a group of Indian women making a tipi.

> When a woman was preparing to make a new lodge . . . she made a feast and to it invited some of her friends . . . When the friends had come and had eaten, she gave to each one a hide and a rope. The different women took them to their homes, wet the hides again, and on the following day softened them, so that all the hides for the lodge might be finished in one day. This was a friendly service, to be repaid in kind as the occasion arose, and was precisely similar to the old-fashioned community barn-raising, quilting, and corn-husking bees [social gatherings] . . .
>
> *Grinnell, The Cheyenne Indians, a written account of his observations of Indian tribes, 1923*

When the hides were tanned they were cut to size and sewn together with buffalo sinew. Cutting and sewing the tipi was also a communal task. When the tipi was finished, it was set up for use. The raising of the tipis was always done by women. First of all, a foundation of 3–4 poles was made by tying the ends together and standing them up. Next the covering was put into place, staked and weighed down with stones.

Tipis were rather like luxurious tents. They were beautifully decorated on the outside by male members of the family. Inside, beds of folded buffalo hides were put at intervals around the edge. *Parfleches* and storage bags were placed between the beds. Water hung in a bag near the door. Wood for the fire was put outside. The floor was often carpeted with buffalo hides. In cold weather a fire built inside the tipi kept everyone warm and comfortable. In hot weather the sides of the tipi were left open to create a cooling breeze. When the Indian band travelled to another camping ground, women supervised the move, dismantled the tipi and packed all the household belongings. For Pretty Shield these moves were exciting occasions:

> A crier would ride through the village telling the people to be ready to move in the morning. In every lodge the children's eyes would begin to shine. Men would sit up to listen, women would go to their doors to hear where the next village would be set up, and then there would be glad talking until it was time to go to sleep. Long before the sun came, the fires would be going in every lodge, the horses, hundreds of them, would come thundering in, and then everybody was very busy. Down would come the lodges, packs would be made, travois loaded. HO! Away we would go, following the men, to some new camping ground, with our children playing around us. It was good hard work to get things packed up, and moving; and it was hard, fast work to get them in shape again, after we camped.
>
> *Frank Linderman, Pretty Shield, oral account, 1932*

Food and cooking

Most of the meat eaten by the Indians was buffalo, provided by the men. Parts of the buffalo such as the brain, the gristle around the nose and the tongue were thought to be really delicious. Buffalo, however, was not their only food. Many of the foods that we eat today came from the Indians. For instance, potatoes, peanuts, tomatoes and corn were all grown by Indian women for centuries.

Traditional American food such as pumpkin pie, maple syrup, cranberry sauce and even the Thanksgiving turkey also came from the Indians. So, of course, did tobacco.

During the winter months when little fresh food was available, people relied on preserved foods. Plains Indians could not freeze nor can their food, so they dried their vegetables, fruits and meats instead. Peppers were dried whole and used to flavour winter foods. *Okra* was cut in slices, spread out to dry and added to soups. Green beans were strung out to dry, and fruit such as peaches and apples were sliced very thinly and put out to dry on the tipi roof. Meat was also sliced thinly and beaten thoroughly before it was hung out for, perhaps, several days. Pretty Shield describes how Indian women preserved their food:

> We first cut up the meat, taking it off the animal in the sections that naturally divide it. Then we split these sections, and spread the meat on racks in the sun, turning it often. At night we took the meat off the racks, piled it on the ground, covered the pile with a buffalo robe, and then trampled upon it to squeeze out all the blood that might yet be in the meat. When morning came again we spread the meat in the sunshine.
>
> *Frank Linderman, Pretty Shield, oral account, 1932*

Pemmican was also stored. This was boiled meat which was pounded very hard, mixed with berries or bits of fat to make it tasty, and made into *patties*. These patties were sometimes put in skin containers to eat in the hard winter months. This description shows us how pemmican was made.

> We cut good, lean meat into strips and dried it a little; then roasted it until it looked brown. After this was done we pounded the dry meat with stone hammers that are found nearly everywhere . . . Next we soaked ripe chokeberries in water, and then used this water to boil crushed bones. When the kettle of boiled bones was cool, we skimmed off the grease from the bone-marrow, mixed it with the pounded meat, poured this into buffalo heart-skins, and let it get solid.
>
> *Frank Linderman, Pretty Shield, oral account, 1932*

Most Indians ate plain meals which used very few spices or herbs. Salt was rarely used, although sometimes meals were made tasty by seasoning with peppermint leaves, wild ginger, or maple syrup. Travelling around such a lot meant that cooking had to be kept simple. One Indian woman, Sarah Winnemucca, describes how food was cooked without ovens:

> Cooking is performed in willow baskets woven so tight as to hold water. Seeds are ground between two stones. A fire is built, and small stones are thrown into it. When hot, these are dropped into the basket that contains the water, causing it to boil, when the meal is stirred in, and hot rocks continually thrown in until the mush is cooked. Meat or stews and soup is cooked in the same manner.
>
> *Oral account*

Indian women gathering wild rice

How Indians obtained their food

Men of each tribe hunted for meat to bring back for the women to cook and preserve. All the other food eaten was either grown, picked or dug up by women. Prickly pears were collected in parfleche bags. Different types of berries were picked. Root vegetables, especially the wild turnip, were dug up using a long, thin, pointed pole called a root-digger. Women thrust the pointed end of their stick hard into the ground to uncover the turnips. Considerable force was sometimes necessary because the soil was often extremely hard. It was hot, heavy and tiring work made easier by working together. Sarah Winnemucca tells of all the different types of food gathered by women.

> We gather the nuts for the winter. This was our principal food, which our women commenced to gather about the middle of August. Our men used to hunt, and after that, our women go into the valleys to gather different kinds of seeds . . . and when the roots begin to grow, the women dig them up. The name of this root in Indian is called yah-bah, and tastes like carrots. They boil them, like potatoes, and use them in soups, and also dry them. Another root is called camas-root, a little root that looks like chestnuts; and root, which tastes a little like hard bread.
>
> *Autobiographical account from the late 19th century*

Some Indian groups, such as the Hidatsa, settled down in the summer months and grew crops such as corn. Corn was grown by the Indians some 10,000 years before white people arrived. It was picked, husked and harvested by women. Maxi'Diwiac describes how women worked hard:

> We Hidatsa women were early risers in the planting season; it was my habit to be up before sunrise, while the air was cool, for we thought this the best time for garden work. Did young men work in the fields? (Laughing heartily) Certainly not! The young men should be off hunting, or on a war party; and youths not yet young men should be out guarding the horses. Their duties were elsewhere, also they spent a great deal of time dressing up to be seen by the village maidens; they should not be working in the fields.
>
> *Oral account, 1917*

Marriage and the family

Many of the Indian groups lived in extended families. Grandparents, aunts, uncles and cousins, as well as mother, father, brother and sister all lived together. They did not all share the same tipi but pitched their homes next to each other. This family group was called a band. Everyone knew each other very well. Being lonely was not a problem for most Indians.

When a Cheyenne man married, he went to live with his wife's family. Men were allowed to have more than one wife in many Indian groups. This was because there were more women than men as a result of losses in war. When a man died, in many tribes his brother married his widow. Mr Grinnell talks about Indian marriages:

> Descent was *matrilineal.* A woman born into the group remained all her life a member of that group, and her children were members of it. When a man married a girl he went to live with her group . . . His children belonged to their mother's group, and not to his own . . . When the woman's sons grew up and married, each went to live with his wife's group . . . A man might live in several groups during his life, a woman in but one.
>
> *Grinnell, The Cheyenne Indians, a written account, 1923*

Not surprisingly, in some tribes women had great influence. Unlike many European women of the time, Cheyenne women felt free to discuss and argue with their husbands about tribal matters. Older women were respected for their wisdom and knowledge, and taught younger women the ways of their tribe. Children were looked after by these wise women who taught them good manners and behaviour proper to a well-brought-up Indian girl or boy.

Children were much wanted, loved, well-treated and cared for by everyone in the camp. Adults very rarely scolded their children. It was never known for an Indian woman to hit her child. Many Indians thought it was strange that white people of this time beat their children but were kind to their animals. Indians were kind to their children but were more willing to beat their animals.

Women's societies

Both men and women had their own societies within each Indian group. One of the most important societies within the Cheyenne was the *quilling* society. Quills were obtained from the porcupine and were dyed in different colours. Yellow was obtained from *huckleberry* root, red from *snakeberry*, blue from clay. Using these variously coloured quills, women decorated bags, shirts, baby carriers and robes. Quilling was delicate work needing patience and nimble fingers.

Fighting women

Hunting and fighting were considered men's jobs. Even so, women were still expected to help their men in battle. In the Sioux nation, bravery was still considered to be the most important virtue for both sexes. (Courage, Fortitude, Generosity and Wisdom were the four most important virtues of the Sioux.) Apache women showed their courage when they rounded up the horses as the men attacked their enemies. Before Blackfoot women became mothers, they often joined their husbands on horse raids. Many Crow women took an active part in warfare. A few women boasted of their coups, just as men did. Some exceptional women took on a fighting role, perhaps to revenge the death of a family member, or because of a religious vision, or just because they wanted to. Pretty Shield, a Crow Indian, recounted how a woman had led a counter-attack against the Sioux. In this incident, a group of Sioux men had attacked the Crow tribe just as the women were putting up the tipis for a new camp. Some Crow men were around but it was a woman who defeated the invaders.

> Now I shall have to tell you about the fighting, a little, because it was a woman's fight. A woman won it. The men never tell about it. They do not like to hear about it, but I am going to tell you what happened . . . There was shooting . . . A Dacota bullet struck a pole, and whined. Arrows were coming among the lodges . . . Several horses were wounded and were screaming with their pain . . . I saw Strikes-two, a woman sixty years old, riding

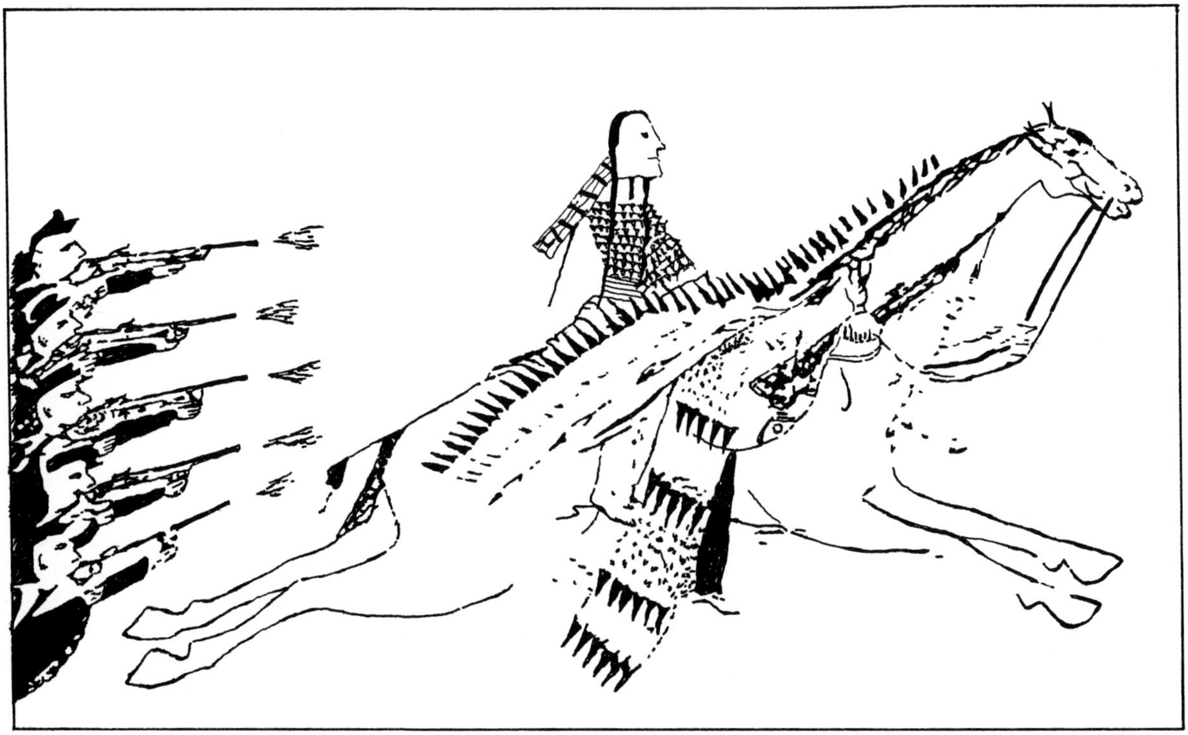

This Buffalo Calf Woman is escaping from the U.S. cavalry

around the camp on a grey horse. She carried her root-digger, and she was singing her medicine song, as though Dacota bullets and arrows were not flying around her . . . She rode out straight at the Dacota, waving her root-digger and singing that song. I saw her, I heard her, and my heart swelled because she was a woman.

Frank Linderman, Pretty Shield, an oral account, 1932

A few women became celebrated warriors. One Gross Ventre girl, who had been taken prisoner by the Crows, grew up to be an excellent horse woman who could shoot and hunt well. When a raiding party of Blackfeet attacked her new home, she fought bravely and well. Five of these Blackfeet men signalled for a peace, so she went out to meet them. When they dared to attack her, she killed one with her gun, wounded two others, leaving the remaining two to run away. From then on she was called Woman Chief. A year later Woman Chief led a group of men warriors against the Blackfeet and succeeded in stealing 70 of their horses. After this she was permitted to sit in Crow war councils. In warrior ceremonies she would tell of more coups than men.

Perhaps the most famous of all woman fighters was Buffalo Calf Woman. Born around 1850, Buffalo Calf Woman, member of the Cheyenne tribe, fought with Indian soldiers at the Battle on the Rosebud River, 17 June 1876. It seems that Buffalo Calf Woman became famous as a warrior because she saved her brother, Comes-In-Sight, when he was trapped by enemy fire. Bravely, she rode directly into the flying bullets to rescue him whilst the other men stood by watching. The Cheyenne named the battle 'The Battle Where the Girl Saved Her Brother' in recognition of her courage. When General Custer was defeated at the Battle of the Little Big Horn, a week later, Buffalo Calf Woman was there fighting alongside the men. As a result of this, the Cheyenne gave her the honorary name of Brave Woman. Buffalo Calf Woman eventually died of diptheria in June 1879 after many other skirmishes with the army.

These women were exceptional. In most Indian groups, women and men had strictly defined roles. Although there was a strong sexual division of labour within all Plains Indian groups, women were not always considered inferior. Indian women were not just drudges at the beck and call of their menfolk but a respected element within the Indian community. Mutual help, support and respect were essential if the Indian group was to survive in such a hostile climate as the Plains.

2 Crossing the Plains

At first the Plains were little more than a highway from the eastern states of the USA to the fertile lands of the far West. No one in their right mind ever thought of settling down in this wild, desolate landscape of the Plains.

Families, friends and others all joined up together to cross the Plains in wagons to make their home in Oregon or California. Between 1840 and 1870 about a quarter of a million Americans crossed over the prairies.

It was approximately 3,500 kilometres (about 2,200 miles) from the Missouri river to California. Journeys of this distance usually took well over four months. Travellers began their adventure early in May or late April. To leave earlier or later could be dangerous. If people started their journey too early there would not be enough prairie grass for their cattle and horses to eat. If they started too late, they might get caught in blizzards and snow. Either way they might not survive.

This hazardous journey was expensive; it cost between 500 and 1,000 dollars for the wagon and supplies. Everything a family needed was packed on board the wagon. Food, furniture and sentimental items were squashed in a small, canvas-covered vehicle. Enough food to last the journey was essential. In 1845 the *emigrants'* Guide to Oregon and California said that emigrants should have a supply of 200 pounds of flour, 150 pounds of bacon, 10 pounds of coffee, 20 pounds of sugar, and 10 pounds of salt. Chipped beef, rice, tea, dried beans, dried fruit, vinegar, and *tallow* for soap and candles were also recommended. Emigrants needed at least a kettle, frying pan, coffee pot, tin plates, cups, knives and forks. A rifle and shot were also necessary. Often wagons were piled high with goods the family thought essential, some to be abandoned later on when the laden wagon moved too slowly.

The decision to move West was not taken

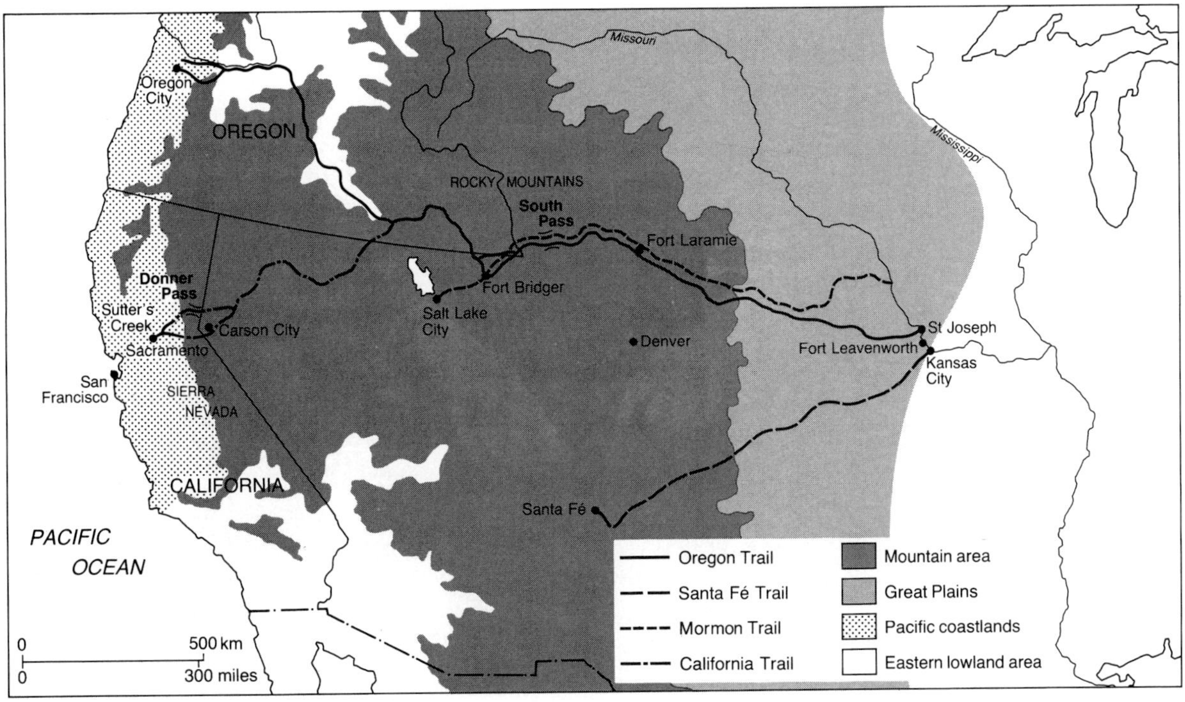

Wagon trails of the pioneer travelling West in the mid 19th century

lightly. Some women, such as Lavinia Porter, were persuaded by their husbands to go in search of a new and richer future:

> I never recall that sad parting from my dear sister on the plains of Kansas without the tears flowing fast and free . . . We were the eldest of a large family, and the bond of affection and love that existed between us was strong indeed . . . as she with the other friends turned to leave me for the ferry which was to take them back to home and civilization, I stood alone on that wild prairie. Looking westward I saw my husband driving slowly over the plain; turning my face once more to the east, my dear sister's footsteps were fast widening the distance between us. For the time I knew not which way to go, nor whom to follow, but in a few moments I rallied my forces . . . and soon overtook the slowly moving oxen who were bearing my husband and child over the green prairie . . . the unbidden tears would flow, in spite of my brave resolve to be the courageous and valiant frontierswoman.

Lavinia Porter, autobiographical account, 1910

For some women like Lulu Fuhr, the sorrow of parting soon gave way to hope and happiness:

> To say I wept bitterly would but faintly express the ocean of tears I shed on leaving my beloved home and state to take up residence in the 'Wild and Wooly West'. However, my fears vanished as we travelled towards our Mecca . . . we felt that instead of the Wild West we had found God's own country and were quite content to accept it as our future home.

Lulu Fuhr, an autobiography, late 19th century

Work on the journey

Journeys across the Plains were long and tedious. Both women and men worked hard throughout the journey. On the first part of the trail they worked at different tasks. The men looked after the travelling arrangements and the women looked after the cooking, aired the beds, cleaned out the wagons and sewed any torn spots in the canvas or in clothing. Women's work took nearly all their waking hours, as Helen Carpenter, a pioneer, notes in her diary:

Exhausted by the journey, this family is taking a midday rest

The plain fact of the matter is, we have no time for sociability. From the time we get up in the morning, until we are on the road, it is hurry scurry to get breakfast and put away the things that necessarily had to be pulled out last night – while, under way, there is no room in the wagon for a visitor, nooning is barely long enough to eat a cold bite – and at night all the cooking utensils and provisions are to be gotten about the camp fire, and cooking enough to last until the next night.

Helen Carpenter, manuscript diary, 1857

As the journey progressed, both men and women did similar jobs. There was no time to say that work was either men's work or women's work. Everyone lent a hand. Women drove wagons, forded streams of ice-cold water, and looked after the cattle whenever it was necessary. Women gained independence that they would not have had if they had stayed back in the East. However, this limited freedom arose from necessity rather than changing attitudes. Although women did take over jobs usually done by men, it was not considered lady-like. When one young woman, proud of her new-found skill in driving a wagon, overheard a conversation between her mother and father, her confidence floundered:

Now while out at the wagon we kept trying until I was fairly successful. How my heart bounded a few days later when I chanced to hear father say to mother, 'Do you know that Mary Ellen is beginning to crack the whip?' Then how it fell again when mother replied, 'I am afraid it isn't a very lady-like thing for a girl to do.' After this, while I felt a secret joy in being able to have a power that set things going, there was also a sense of shame over this new accomplishment.

Mary Ellen Hixon, a young pioneer, autobiography, late 19th century

Health and hazards

To breathe in fresh pure air every day was no doubt good for the health. By 1860, however, trail conditions, were unpleasant. Water was polluted, trail-sites were full of litter, waste and toilet remains making some parts of the Plains very smelly. In 1853, one pioneer, Charlotte Pengra, reported 'an unendurable stench that rose from a ravine that is resorted to for special purposes by all the Emigration'. Basic privacy was difficult especially for women. Women escorted each other out behind the wagon train, making a circle with their skirts to protect each other from prying eyes. Rags were tied or pinned in place when a woman menstruated and were later washed out as privately as possible. With scarce water, a poor diet and insanitary conditions, many people suffered and died from *dysentry*, *cholera* and *typhoid*.

Life was dangerous in other ways. Swirling rivers had to be crossed, torrential rain had to be driven through, as one woman wrote in her diary:

Crossing the Deschutres River, the women took their places in the boats, feeling they were facing death . . . the frail craft would get caught in a whirlpool and the water dashing over and drenching them through and through. The men would then plunge in the cold stream and draw the half-drowned women and children ashore, build fires and partly dry them, and the bedding, and start on again. The women preferring to try it afoot, but that was no pleasure trip, carrying a small child in arms whilst another one or two clung to their skirts whilst they climbed over fallen trees and rocks.

Nancy Hembree, A Snow Bogart Reminiscences of a Journey Across the Plains in 1843, diary extract

Storms were very violent on the Plains, as Amelia Stewart Knight, one brave pioneer, vividly noted at the time:

We had a dreadful storm of rain and hail last night and very sharp lightning. It killed two oxen for one man. We had just encamped on a large flat prairie, when the storm commenced in all its fury and in two minutes, after the cattle were taken from the wagons, every brute was gone out of sight, cows, calves, horses, all gone before the storm like so many wild beasts. I never saw such a storm. The wind was so high I thought it would tear the wagons to pieces. Nothing but the stoutest covers could stand it. The rain beat into the wagons so that everything was wet, in less than 2 hours the water was a foot deep all over our camp grounds. As we could have no tents pitched, all had to crowd into the wagons and sleep in wet beds with their wet clothes on without supper. The wind blew hard all night and this morning presents a dreary prospect surrounded by water . . .

Amelia Stewart Knight, Diary of an Oregon Pioneer, 1853

Part of a poster advertising the opening of the first railroad to run from the East to the West coast

The dream of exploring new territory soon faded away as the grim reality of life aboard a wagon train was realised. Some of these pioneers did eventually reach their destination. After a few hard months journeying across unknown territory, the travellers settled down into their new homes in the far West, leaving their memories of the plains far behind.

Railways

Travelling across the Plains became a lot easier once the railway network, known as the railroad or the iron horse, was expanded. Before the 1860s the railroads stopped at the Mississippi–Missouri rivers. When Willianna Hickman travelled with her husband and six children to the all-black settlement at Nicodemus, the railroad left them in Ellis with thirty miles to go:

> We left there for Nicodemus, travelling overland with horses and wagons. We were two days on the way, with no roads to direct us save deer trails and buffalo wallows. We travelled by compass. At night the men built bonfires and sat around them, firing guns to keep the wild animals from coming near. We reached Nicodemus about 3 o'clock on the second day.
>
> *Willianna Hickman talking about her experiences in 1878 in Dorothy Sterling, We Are Your Sisters: Black Women in the Nineteenth Century, 1984*

By the 1890s railroads ran from coast to coast across the Plains. This provided a fairly cheap, easy and safe way to travel West. People were encouraged to make the journey. As well as advertising in the USA, railway companies advertised in northern European countries such as England, France and Denmark to encourage people to settle in America . . . and use the railway.

At first, pioneers were keen to leave the Plains behind them to travel to the richer lands of the Far West. However, you will see in the next chapter how this situation changed.

Other forms of transport became popular on the Plains. These travellers are waiting for the Mississippi riverboat, 1897

3 Homesteading women

Up until the 1840s, the Plains were known as the Great American Desert. Water, wood and good soil were hard to find, and the weather was terrible. In summer the temperature soared above 100°C, yet in winter dropped to −40°C. On top of this, the wind blew all the time. Not surprisingly, white settlers had no wish to live on this land. For centuries Indians had lived on the Plains. But times were changing. Land elsewhere in America was becoming scarce and expensive. At first the government did not allow white people to live on the Plains, but by the 1860s they had bought Kansas and Nebraska from the Indians and were keen to encourage white settlement. The government disliked the idea of having settlements in the East and West of America and only Indians in the middle. New laws were passed and railways were built to make it easier for pioneers to settle on the Plains.

The Homestead Act

In 1862 the government passed the Homestead Act. This Act allowed anyone over the age of 21 to claim and settle 160 acres of land for free if they lived and worked on it for five years. This Act encouraged many adventurous and independent people to move onto the Plains. The people who took up the government's offer were called homesteaders. The following extract lays down some of the terms of the Act.

> Any person who is the head of a family, or who has arrived at the age of twenty-one years, . . . and is a citizen of the United States, or who shall have filed his declaration of intention to become such . . . and who has never borne arms against the United States Government or given aid and comfort to its enemies shall, from and after the first January eighteen hundred and sixty-three, be entitled to enter one quarter section or a less quantity of unappropriated public lands . . . after the land has been surveyed . . .

Extract from An Act to Secure Homesteads to Actual Settlers on the Public Domain, 20 May 1862

Who were the homesteaders?

Homesteaders came from many different backgrounds. By far the largest group was white American settlers who came from the East in search of cheap land. Farmers, tradespeople, lawyers and politicians all came to farm 'out West'. Black Americans had won their fight against southern slavery in 1863 and some moved to the Plains in search of a

Ho for Kansas!

COME!

To the Colored People of the United States of America:

This is to lay before your minds a few sketches of what great advantages there are for the great mass of people of small means that are emigrating West to come and settle in the county of Hodgeman, in the State of Kansas — and more especially the Colored people, for they are the ones that want to find the best place for climate and for soil for the smallest capital. Hodgeman county is in Southwestern Kansas, on the line of the Atchison, Topeka & Santa Fe Railroad.

We, the undersigned, having examined the above county and found it best adapted to our people, have applied to the proper authority and have obtained a Charter, in the name and style of "THE DAVID CITY TOWN COMPANY," in the County of Hedgeman, State of Kansas.

TRUSTEES

A. McCLURE. STEPHEN ESSEX.
JOHN YATES. THOMAS JACKSON.
THOMAS BIEZER. JOHN GOTHARD.
HENRY BRILEE.

A. McCLURE, President.
J. WOODFORK, Secretary.

An advert encouraging people to settle in Kansas

new life. European families fled to America to escape poverty and unemployment. Times were hard in countries such as England, Ireland, Italy and Russia. These immigrants came to look for new opportunities and realise their dreams of wealth. Other Europeans, such as Jewish people, fled from persecution. They hoped America would provide them with greater freedom. Indians could not take advantage of the Homestead Act because the government did not consider them to be U.S. citizens. As the white settler moved in, so the Indian was pushed out.

At first people settled in Kansas, Nebraska and Minnesota but after 1880 they spread out to the rest of the land in Colorado, Wyoming and the Dakotas.

Although most homesteaders were family groups, about 10% were single women. Research by Dick Everett, an historian, illustrates this:

> Contrary to expectation, a noteworthy proportion of the first settlers were single or unattached women. These were especially noticeable in a land of hardship. They tried without training or physical strength to wrest a living where strong men had great difficulty in maintaining their hold. Many were sensitive, delicate, cultured women, unused to the harsh work involved in conquering the Plains. They were plucky and staunch, taking things as they came, in an uncomplaining manner.
>
> *Dick Everett, Sod House Frontier, 1943*

Although the homesteaders came from many different backgrounds, their daily lives were mostly very similar. For most homesteaders this new and barren land offered great opportunities if they worked long and hard.

Initially they were often overawed by the desolate landscape. There was nothing there. It was a land of wide open spaces without houses, shops or transport. Lydia Murphy, an early settler on the Plains, recalls her first impressions of this new land:

> It was such a new world, reaching to the far horizon without break of tree or chimney stack; just sky and grass and grass and sky . . . The hush was so loud. As I lay in my unplastered upstairs' room, the heavens seemed nearer than ever before and awe and beauty and mystery over all.
>
> *Lydia Murphy, autobiography, 1859*

It needed great depth of character and courage to cope with the emptiness of the wide open Plains which seemed unending. One mother became so desperate for company that she lay down with her sheep for warmth and reassurance when she was alone all day.

Building a home

When the homesteaders arrived on their land, they first built a temporary home, then a permanent one. Temporary homes were made from whatever material the settlers had brought with them. This was usually a canvas tent or a hut made from sheets of *zinc*. Zinc homes were very uncomfortable to live in, especially in the hot weather. The sides of zinc houses were so hot in the summer months that you could bake bread on the walls!

For a more permanent home the homesteaders relied on whatever natural material they found. In some places they were lucky because there were rocks or trees to build stone houses or log cabins. On drier parts of the prairies, homesteaders were not so lucky, for there was nothing but soil. So they built houses by cutting the dry earth into bricks. These earth bricks were called sods and the houses built from them called soddies.

Soddies took about three weeks to build, with all the family lending a hand. Men, women and children all helped to stack the layers of sod bricks. Thick lumps of the prairie sod were laid grass side down and put side by side to make walls of about one metre thick. Any hole that appeared was filled with dirt or mud. The roof was built on wooden poles and covered with dung.

Although soddies were warm in winter and cool in summer and rarely burnt down, they were definitely not luxury homes. Most sod houses only had one room about five metres by six metres in which the family ate, drank and slept. All sorts of insects and small creatures, from spiders to fleas, from mice to rattle-snakes, made their home in the bricks. They often crawled out to feed on the homesteaders' stores, bringing disease and, in the case of the rattle-snake, instant death. The soddies had few windows and therefore little light and air. Dirt and straw dropped on

Former slaves beginning their new life as landowners

everything. When it rained heavily, the sods started to crumble and muddy water dripped in. All kinds of pots and pans were used in a vain attempt to catch the water. People ill in bed or babies were covered with umbrellas to stop them from getting wet. Cooking became very difficult, as one patient Plains woman recalls:

Sometimes the water would drip on the stove while I was cooking, and I would have to keep tight lids on the *skillets* to prevent mud from falling into the food. With my dress pinned up, and rubbers on my feet, I waded around until the clouds rolled by.

Unknown Plains woman

Soddies were not ideal homes but they were cheap and easy to build. As the homesteader had little money or time, these soddies were very popular. More than 90% of Nebraskan settlers lived in a soddie at one time in their life.

Some families found it easier to build a dugout. This meant digging a home into the side of a hill, leaving small openings for doors and windows. These dugouts were even more uncomfortable than the sod houses. They were damp and dark all the time. The dirt from the roof and walls dropped inside the home, covering furniture, clothing, cooking pots and everything else. It was even worse when it rained. Then the dugout flooded completely and the family had to leave.

Working life

Once the family had a home, they turned their attention to farming the land. The supplies they had brought with them would not last long. Land needed to be ploughed, planted and harvested. Cows, sheep and other livestock needed to be fed and looked after. Labour was scarce, so all members of the family – women, men and children – all worked together to build a new life. Traditional ideas about women quickly vanished due to necessity. The following account by Clara Hildebrand shows us some of the work women were expected to do:

> The pioneer Kansas woman shared her husband's work and interest in the garden, in the orchard, the crops and animals of the farm. She worked in the garden and gathered its products. She knew first how each vineyard or tree in the young orchard was coming on. She shared the hopes for a bountiful crop as the field things sprouted and grew green and tall. Did a horse, dog or other farm animal get badly gored, cut or wounded, hers was the task to cleanse the wound and take the stitch that drew the torn edges together.
>
> *Clara Hildebrand, oral interview, 1873 in J. Stratton, Pioneer Women, 1981*

A dugout in Nebraska

A maize field and sod house in Nebraska, 1880s

Women helped with everything, even the ploughing which was traditionally the most strenuous work on the farm and usually reserved for men and oxen. Mrs J. H. O'Loughlin, who settled in Kansas, explained what ploughing and planting involved:

> We prepared the soil for planting with a breaking plough, and then used an axe or hatchet to make a hole in the sod, then dropped the seed and closed the hole with our heels. The ground squirrels got part of our seed but we had very good crops the first year.

Mrs J. H. O'Loughlin, an autobiography, 1879, in J. Stratton, Pioneer Women, 1981

Good harvests were important: if the crops failed, the family starved. Most, if not all, the food eaten was grown on the farm. To ensure that there was always enough to last the year, pioneer women had to be resourceful, well organised and able to plan carefully in advance. Wheat (for bread), potatoes and sweet-corn were the staple diet. Bread-making was a time-consuming process which could take all day, as Miriam Colt shows in her diary:

> Have really labored hard all day, and have baked only two small loaves of bread, while, in a family of seven like ours, one can be dispatched at each meal.

Miriam Colt, diary of a 19th century pioneer

Fresh meat was plentiful in season. Prairie chicken, duck, deer and rabbits were often caught by the homesteading women. In the winter months, the homesteader relied on meat preserved by salting and smoking.

Lack of fresh vegetables was a constant source of worry for many homesteaders because of the risk of *scurvy*. However, one plant which looked like an onion, called the camas root, was eaten regularly. It was very sweet and tasted like figs. Many wild fruits also grew on the Plains, so the wise pioneer woman preserved as many as she could. Sometimes this meant using unconventional methods such as cooking the wild fruit until it was like a thin paste, sieving it and drying it on large plates until it looked like leather.

It was mainly left to the women and children to collect buffalo dung for fuel, which was then stored in a dry corner of the house.

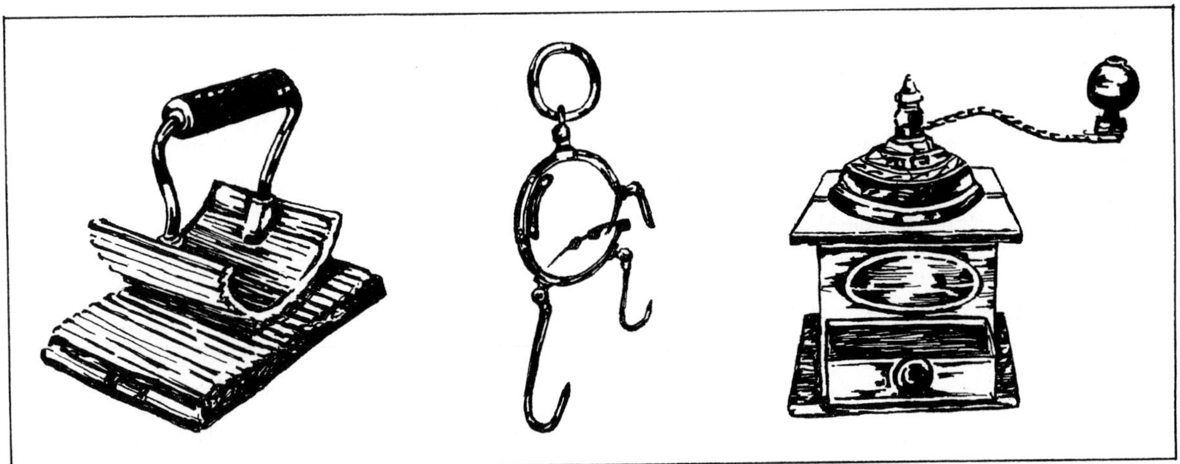

A homesteader's household utensils. Using a time-saving fluting iron, a woman could keep ruffles in her simple calicoes. A portable scale could weigh anything from a bucket of feed to a side of beef. Coffee and things like rye were hand ground in this box mill

Cow chips, as they were known, burnt very quickly and cooking food was therefore hard work. Many women were very particular about hygiene at first and often used wooden sticks to put the dung in the fire. Later they used their hands, washing them afterwards. Sometimes they did not even have the time or the energy to do that.

Daily housework often took up much of a woman's time, and she spent many long and tedious hours cooking, cleaning, sewing and laundering. There was no running water, so water needed for drinking, cooking and cleaning was carried from a nearby river or well. Washing was usually taken down to the river. Miriam Davis Colt, a Kansas pioneer, wrote in her diary how they had to 'make do':

> May 19th: Mrs V, Sister L and self, have been to the creek and done up our last month's washing. Had the inconveniences of hard water, a scanty supply of soap . . . Starching and ironing will be dispensed with . . . A rub through the hand is all my own and the children's clothes can have, and the same will be done to their papa's linen.
>
> *Miriam Davis Colt, Kansas pioneer, 19th century*

Women could not run down to the corner shop if they ran out of household goods. Everything had to be made at home well in advance. Even basic essentials such as candles and soap were made by women. Making soap was a difficult process which took several weeks. Emeline Crumb, a homesteader in Kansas, describes the soap-making process:

> Soap-making was a complicated matter . . . All the grease and scraps of fat trimmings that had been collected during the year were brought to the place (backyard) . . . when thoroughly cooked, water was put in a wooden tub and the mess turned in and set aside to cool. The debris settled in the bottom, and mushy grease on top was partly made soap.
>
> *Emeline Crumb, oral account, 19th century*

Life often seemed to be work, work and more work, with no time or opportunity for leisure. Perhaps the life of many women could be summed up in the words of this pioneer, who lived in Texas:

> This was a little of my day: When you first get up in the morning, before daybreak, you start your fire . . . and put your coffee on. Then, just as it is getting light over the hills, you go after the calves. When you bring back the calves, you milk the cows; then bring the calves to their mother cows. Leaving them for a while, you fix breakfast, which is a big meal. After breakfast, at a time when people are getting up in the cities nowadays, you skim the milk and make the butter, feed the dogs, cats and the hogs . . . and turn the calves in their pasture and the cows in theirs. When the butter is made and the dishes washed, the house spic and span, you go to help in the fields. The woman leaves the little baby at the edge of the field with a quilt put above it so the sun won't harm it. When the baby cries the woman leaves the hoe or the plow and goes to it to tend it or nurse it. Then she goes back to the plow or her work in the field. There was usually a little baby or several small children at a time. When the sun is in the middle of the sky it is time for dinner.

The woman leaves for the house and prepares the food. After eating, the men might lay down for a little while to rest, but there is no rest for the women. There is always work to be done. In the afternoon there may be more work in the fields, or baking, candlemaking, soap-making, sewing, mending, any of the hundred pressing tasks, and then the calves must again be rounded up and brought home, as the shadows fall the cows milked, the chickens fed, always something, early and late.

Mathilda Wagner, Texas pioneer, diary extract, 19th century

Problems on the prairie

Whilst everyday life was hard enough, there were other problems that homesteaders faced on the Plains. Floods and droughts endangered crops and livestock. In 1860 a long drought affected Kansas. Fifteen months went by without a drop of rain. Animals collapsed on the ground panting for water. Crops withered in the field.

Winters were sometimes very harsh too. Water froze in breakfast mugs and bread had to be thawed, a slice at a time, by the fire. Snow fell through the leaky roofs inches deep, soaking the furniture and bedding. Blizzards were even worse. These were ice-dust wind storms which blew across the Plains, freezing animals and even people.

Rainstorms could also be devastating, as Emma Mitchell, a Kansas pioneer, discovered:

A terrible storm and cloudburst came upon us and we lost almost everything, except the cows and an old team in the pasture . . . we discovered our cellar was full of water from the outside door, and the well curb and toilet were gone. The creek was up to the house and still pouring down. My husband investigated and found that the underpinning of the house was going and that we had to get out . . . We stayed until the storm abated and the water went down . . . We couldn't shut the door when we left the house, so the kitchen was full of rubbish, and everything had been swimming in the high water. Many things were upside down. When the water went down, there was an inch of mud all over the carpets and floors. When the daylight came, it was a sad sight to behold. Our cow-barn and ponies were swept away, also our sack of millett. Practically everything we had was gone or ruined: machinery, wagons and nice garden . . . Our ponies washed downstream about sixteen miles.

Emma Mitchell, autobiography, 1877

Grasshoppers were another hazard which destroyed the crops amongst other things. In August 1874 in Kansas, grasshoppers ate everything in sight including the crops, wooden furniture and even clothes. Adelheit Weits, a settler in Kansas, described her own awful experience:

The storm of grasshoppers came one Sunday. I remember that I was wearing a dress of white with a green stripe. The grasshoppers settled on me and ate up every bit of green stripe in that dress before anything could be done about it.

Adelheit Weits, autobiography, 1867

Three prairie women in traditional working clothes.

Medicine and health

Women were not only involved in domestic and farm chores but were usually responsible for the health of the family. For the homesteaders, disease was one of their greatest enemies. Cholera, *malaria*, smallpox, typhoid, *pleurisy* and *pneumonia* were rife. Disease spread quickly due to an unbalanced diet and poor living conditions. Qualified doctors were few, hospitals almost unheard of and medical supplies very difficult to obtain. So the responsibility of caring and providing for the sick fell to the women in the community.

Women often found themselves surprisingly skilled in their mastery of herbs, bone setting and delivery of children. Most women had a stock of folk remedies for various illnesses and were used to helping in childbirth and laying out the dead. Recipes for remedies were often scribbled down on the back of notebooks and diaries and were passed down through generations. Women used wild herbs and roots, brewed in teas or put on the body as poultices. They found that salt made a reasonable toothpaste and gunpowder could be applied to warts. *Turpentine* was used to clean open cuts, as was lard, goose grease, and even skunk oil. A popular cure for snake bites was to put chicken flesh on the bite to help draw out the poison.

When accidents occurred, women treated the injured with whatever resources they had. Amy M. Loucks, reminiscing in 1879, said that she had always been interested in medicine, even though she had had no formal training. With no more than a fiddle string and an ordinary needle, she stitched back the scalp of a man. She removed a bullet from another man and amputated three fingers from the crushed hand of a railroad man with a razor and a pair of embroidery scissors.

Contraception and contraceptive advice was virtually non-existent at this time. What little there was rarely filtered through to the women of the West and the Plains. Many believed that when breast feeding they could not get pregnant. Today we know that this is not the case. So, once married, they began the endless cycle of conception, birth and child-rearing, frequently having one in the cradle, one at the breast and one on the way.

Giving birth was often a lonely process. Many women gave birth on their own, without the help of a doctor, midwife or even a friend. Mrs A. S. Lecleve gave birth to her third child with only her four-year-old and her eighteen-month-old for company. Her husband had gone out for the day in search of firewood and her nearest neighbour was 3 miles away. Her daughter retells the experience:

Large families were common

My brave mother got the baby clothes together on a chair by the bed, water and scissors and what else was needed to take care of the baby; drew a bucket of fresh water from a 60′ well: made some bread and butter sandwiches and set out some milk for the babies. And when Rover had orders to take care of the babies he never let them out of his sight, for at that time any bunch of weeds might harbour a rattlesnake . . . At about noon the stork left a fine baby boy.

Mrs Lecleve, oral interview, late 19th century

Due to necessity, women worked right up until the moment of birth. Mary Walker, a mother of eight, tells how she fitted childbirth into her daily routine:

Rose about five. Had breakfast. Got my housework done about 9. Baked 6 loaves of bread. Made a kettle of mush and have now a suet pudding and beef boiling. I have managed to put my house in order. May the merciful be with me through the unexpected scene. Nine o'clock p.m. was delivered of another son.

Mary Walker, a diary extract, late 19th century

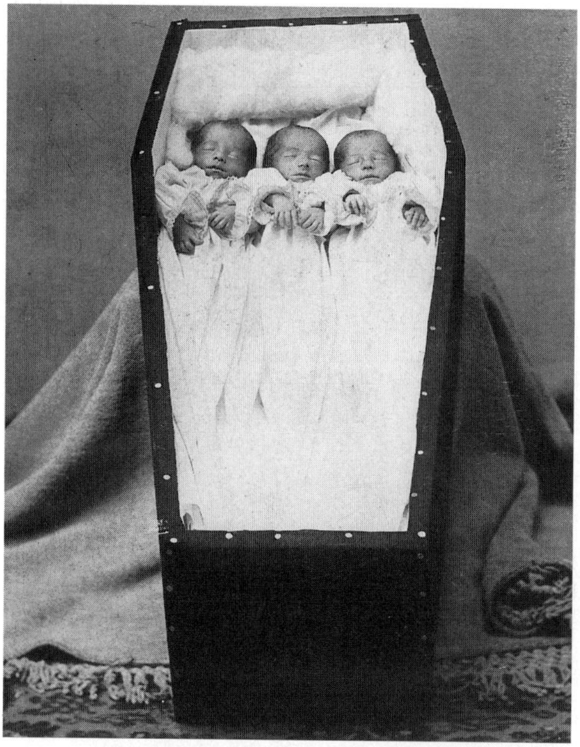

Many children did not survive the harsh conditions of the Plains. This photograph, taken around 1880, would have been cherished by the family and probably placed on the mantelpiece

Most families were large. This was partly because contraception was not widely used, but also because children were highly valued and they could help with the daily work. Younger children carried water and buffalo chips to the home, whilst the older ones helped with the planting and harvesting.

Although girls mostly helped their mothers and boys their fathers, all children helped with the heavy work when needed.

Social life

As more and more people settled on the Plains, life became less lonely. People now had neighbours for company and work was not the only activity, as Mary Lyon, a Kansas pioneer, recalls:

Don't think that all our time and thoughts were taken up with the problem of living. We were a social people. We never waited for an introduction or invitation to be neighbourly.

Mary Lyon, Kansas pioneer, autobiography, 1872

Visiting was an opportunity for the adults to compare notes and the children to play and listen to stories. Travellers were always made welcome, particularly those from the East who brought news.

Some families met regularly. In North Dakota in the 1870s, for example, eight families held dances, rotating them between their houses, every Friday night. In the summer picnics were a favourite pastime. They were often a local affair. Each family packed baskets of food containing bread and butter, fried prairie chicken, boiled ham, pickles and other delicacies. All this had been grown and cooked on their farm.

Women also met each other at '*bees*'. There were *quilting* bees, *husking* bees, apple bees and *fulling* bees. On these occasions women made quilts, husked vegetables, processed fruit or produced cloth. It gave them a chance to meet and talk together whilst they worked.

Families also met up at religious services. They came together to worship, pray and offer each other support. Weddings were a very special occasion and gave all the local people an opportunity to stop work, sometimes for several days.

There were at least two holidays a year which involved everyone. Decoration Day

These women are at a bee in North Dakota. What are they doing?

welcomed Spring and gave everyone the opportunity to remember their dead by picking flowers and decorating the graves. Afterwards they had a picnic. Everyone celebrated the 4th of July which was Independence Day. This was the day America had won her independence from Britain in 1776. Celebrations included flag-waving and speeches, horse races, sack races, foot races and basketball. There was music, singing and fireworks and dancing well into the night.

Nevertheless, life was not always a social whirlpool. Whilst many determined women built new lives on the Plains, not all women could cope with the strain. Some found life on the Plains too harsh and returned to the East. For instance, Victoria, a small town in Kansas, where many wealthy English people had settled in the early 1870s, was deserted by 1878. Others died young. Mrs Seth and her four children from Glasgow, for example, died of fever soon after their arrival, leaving behind a husband and a son.

In order to survive on the Plains, families had to put up with many hardships. The women whose accounts survived showed courage, determination and an amazing ability to adapt to their environment.

4 Independent women

A woman's place . . . ?

For some women, pioneering meant more than just setting up home on the Plains or in the West. It was to provide them with the opportunity to break free from the restricting role of 'Victorian womanhood'.

According to the middle- and upper-class ideal of women in the 19th century, a perfect woman was one who was devoted to the care and attention of her husband and children. For the unmarried woman, this devotion was to be directed towards a good cause serving the community. Whilst many women did do paid work and had to work to make ends meet, it was usually considered improper for upper- and middle-class women to earn a living. Women were not allowed to vote, involve themselves in politics or argue with their husbands. They did not have any legal rights to either their possessions or their children. Upon marriage, the Victorian woman became part of her husband's belongings. Unmarried women, viewed as unfortunate beings, had their affairs looked after by a male relative. It was simply not seemly for women to be seen to be independent. The ideal woman was feminine in dress and thought, and relied entirely on the men in her family to direct her life.

Most women's lives in Britain at this time did not fit this ideal perfectly. Even so, this notion of the perfect Victorian woman was transported to America by *immigrants*, through newspapers and the widespread influence of British ideas. As the towns of the West and the Plains grew, it was inevitable that these Victorian ideas would spread. There were many people of both sexes in the West, as well as the East, who agreed that a woman's place was in the home.

Company H, in 1890, was one of several all-female companies brought into service on special occasions to form a parade

The Madonna of the prairie *by W.H.D. Koerner. This is an idealised picture. Notice the way in which the canvas forms a halo around her head. This woman is neatly dressed and calm, patiently awaiting her fate as mother. Courtesy of the Buffalo Bill Historical Center, Cody, Wyoming*

Despite these Victorian values, women in the West and on the Plains had greater freedom and opportunities than those on the East coast. At first, this was borne out of necessity due to the shortage of labour, but gradually attitudes towards women did change.

Newly built towns on the Plains and in the West attracted independent women with aims and ambitions of their own, who were willing to break away from the traditional role.

Working in the West and on the Plains

Women had always worked both inside and outside the home. Women cooked in restaurants, took in laundry and kept home for single men. A number of women went to work in shops, often serving as post mistresses and mail clerks. Many women became seamstresses, dress-makers or milliners. They ran and sometimes owned hotels.

A photographer from Oregon, advertising her skills around 1892

A number of women proved extremely enterprising and ran their own very successful businesses. Sallie Frazier, a black woman, owned a popular restaurant in Dodge City, Kansas. Although Dodge City was known to be a violent, lawless and dangerous place, Sallie Frazier made sure her restaurant remained respectable. No drink, bad language or fighting was allowed. She was quite prepared to enforce these rules herself with the help of her regular customers. She was the only woman listed by the census as having her own business.

In Nevada City, Luzena Wilson set up a restaurant, doing the actual building work herself, as she later recalled:

> With my own hands I chopped stakes, drove them into the ground and set up my table. I bought provisions from a neighbouring store, and when my husband came back at night, he found, mid the weird light of the pine torches, twenty men sitting at my table.
>
> *Luzena Wilson, oral interview*

Luzena Wilson's business was so successful that she was soon able to build a small hotel and lend money at an interest rate of 10% per month.

Initially laundry services also paid well, especially in the gold-mining towns. Male gold-miners relied on the few women in the towns for domestic service. Prices could be higher here than in other areas.

Clara Brown, who had once been a slave, washed shirts and invested the profits. Living in Colorado she soon amassed $10,000 which she used to find her daughter who had been sold as a slave. The remainder she put towards helping other ex-slaves find work.

Some women learnt from their husbands and were often able to take over their businesses if need be. Mrs Downing, whose husband was the editor of a Kansas paper, *The Ellis County Star*, contributed to his work in a number of ways by setting type, folding papers and doing many other jobs involved in the publication of a weekly newspaper.

Two women setting type for the newspaper, Kansas Workman

Calamity Jane, dressed as a U.S. Army scout

Black Mary, Calamity Jane and Annie Oakley

A few women became legends in their own lifetimes. Black Mary, as she was known, lived in Montana and became the second woman in history to drive a U.S. mail coach. She spent eight years hauling *freight* and was a familiar sight with a cigar clamped between her teeth.

Martha Jane Connary, better known as Calamity Jane, also became a legendary figure. Wearing men's clothes, Calamity Jane used to join the men in the saloon for a drink. Some of her jobs were said to include working as a pony express rider, a wagon freighter and an Indian fighter.

Some women were appalled by Calamity Jane's behaviour. In Dakota, where she worked as a bartender, Calamity Jane recalls how she had to take swift action to avoid:

> . . . the good, virtuous women who planned to turn me out. They came into the bar with a horse whip and shears to cut off my hair. I jumped off the bar and before they could say silken had them bowling.
>
> *Calamity Jane, 19th-century pioneer*

Annie Oakley became a legend in her own time for her expertise with a gun. When her father died, Annie Oakley, only a child herself, supplemented the family income by shooting small animals and birds. Quails and rabbits were sold to local hotels for cash to support the family. Her more notorious career began when she accepted a challenge at a shooting match from a professional, Frankie Butler. She won and they later married. In 1885 they signed on with Buffalo Bill's original Wild West Show. Annie Oakley's fame as a shooting expert grew. Shooting the edge of a playing card from 30 paces and exploding cartridges thrown into the air were her specialities. She could also shoot over her shoulder using a hand mirror to hit her target.

Annie Oakley meets in the mountains with Indian chiefs from several different tribes

These two pictures are of Pearl Hart, a demure lady turned hardened outlaw. She was jailed for five years for holding up a stage coach and stealing 431 dollars

Women and entertainment

Entertainment attracted a number of women from the East. Women were scarce on the frontier, so many men welcomed the opportunity for a share in female company, even at a distance. Women worked across the West and on the Plains as singers, dancers and actresses. Famous names included Lotta Crabtree, an actress who first appeared on the stage at the age of eight, and a Polish actress, Helene Modjeska. Daredevil exploits, such as those performed by these two women in the poster, also got an audience.

These women performed an act called the 'Human Fly'. Their shoes were fitted with special clamps which slotted into holes in the ceiling. It was a dangerous act, and one of the women plunged to her death when the clamps slipped out of the holes

Low wages in other trades forced some women to become prostitutes. Women were sometimes part-time prostitutes in order to supplement their meagre wages from the *sweated trades*. Young girls newly arrived in cities such as Dodge City, Butte and Cripple Creek were easy prey and often found themselves taken in by houses of ill-repute. The existence of this profession exposed the hypocrisy of the Victorian values which many people in the West and on the Plains still held. These women did not fit the Victorian ideal of womanhood but they were seen to serve a necessary function and it was acceptable for men to use them. The large number of single men guaranteed their employment. As these women were outside the Victorian definition of womanhood, it meant that they could curse, drink and smoke in public, unlike other women. However, they were ostracised by both men (even those who used their services) and women.

Nevertheless, people in the West and on the Plains did not live in a totally Victorian society. Women of independent spirit lived their lives to the full and achieved their aims in a way the East would never have tolerated.

Prostitutes outside their home in 'Lousetown' in N. America. Photograph courtesy of the Alaska State Library, P.E. Larss Collection, PCA 41–54

5 Women as community builders

As time went on, the early settlements of the homesteaders grew in size. To begin with, *Congress* controlled local government and what law and order there was. As the population increased, the settlements were given more freedom in choosing their officials, and when an area had 60,000 inhabitants, it could apply to become a member state of the U.S.A. Then it could take responsibility for its own government and finance and could choose its own governor. Each area was keen to receive more settlers so that it could apply for admission. However, they didn't just want ex-convicts or prostitutes; they wanted women as community builders.

Women were brought up to believe that they should take responsibility for the moral and spiritual welfare of their families. The effect of the arrival of women in early communities was quite considerable. They were appalled by the lack of schools, churches and libraries in the towns of the Plains and the West but soon set out to raise money to build them.

Building schools

Education was seen as essential to teach children the values and beliefs of their society.

Breaktime at a school in Kansas in 1899

Sometimes women taught their children at home or one of the women in the community would set up a school for the local children. Emily Biggs did just this, after her own children had left home. Her daughter recalls what she did:

> She searched out her hoarded school books and old school bell, made the versatile flour barrel into a teachers' desk; the goods box, dining table; shoe back, general utility table became students' desks.
>
> *Emily Biggs talking to her daughter, quoted in J. Stratton, Pioneer Women, 1981*

As small communities grew, the residents pooled their resources to employ a teacher. Advertisements were placed in Eastern newspapers to attract young single women to the newly built school-houses. In 1859 the *Lynne County Kansas* printed an advertisement for one hundred school marms, who will pledge themselves not to get married within three years.

Although teaching was open to both men and women, the vast majority of teachers were female. Teaching was one of the few professions open to women at this time and was considered women's work. Low pay and poor working conditions made teaching unattractive to career-minded young men. Parents paid a subscription each month to pay for the teacher's salary. To eke out this small income, teachers usually boarded with the parents of pupils, moving from family to family. Teachers stayed with families with a small number of children for only a short time, whereas families with many children gave hospitality to the teacher for long periods. Olive Owen tells of her experience as a teacher in Kansas in 1857:

> I went around the neighbourhood and gathered the children for a subscription school. The parents couldn't afford much, so I was supposed to board as part of my *remuneration*.
>
> *Olive Owen, autobiography, quoted in J. Stratton, Pioneer Women, 1981*

School facilities were at first sparse and basic. Classrooms were made from empty dugouts or sod cabins. There were few

A sod schoolhouse

blackboards, so the teacher wrote on the dirt floor with a stick. Children sat in rows on logs and benches. One teacher, Anne Webber, who taught at a school in Kansas in 1881, sat on the floor when she needed to use her chair as a table. Most studies were taught by heart because there were few books or teaching resources. Children brought books from home, if they had any, to share with the others.

When communities grew more prosperous they built their own school-house and bought furniture and resources. Emma Handy had taught in five districts in Kansas and found that:

. . . some schools had teachers' desks and chairs, also blackboards and lights.

Emma Handy, autobiography, 1876, quoted in J. Stratton, Pioneer Women, 1981

Despite the rather primitive conditions and resources, and also the youth of the teachers (Katie McGee was 16 when she first started teaching in 1883 and Olive Owen only 15), standards appear to have been good for the time. Nebraska and Kansas had some of the highest literacy rates in the country between 1870 and 1900.

This new public library in Colorado was the pride of the townswomen

The church

Religion was an important part of 19th-century family life. In the early communities, an *itinerant* minister held services whenever he visited each district. For the women of the time this was not sufficient. They were eager to employ their own minister who would look after their spiritual needs every day. Funds were raised through fairs, raffles, picnics and other such activities. When there were sufficient funds, a church was built and a minister appointed. If money was scarce, families donated building materials and helped furnish the interior. Until the church was completed, services were held in private houses, as Effie Thompson of Kansas recalls in the 1840s:

> The scattered families would gather at our home to have Sunday School and hear an occasional circuiteer.
>
> *Effie Thompson, oral account, in J. Stratton, Pioneer Women, 1981*

The congregation of Wichita, Kansas, gather in front of their makeshift log church, 1869

Drink, violence and prohibition

Violence was commonplace in the new towns of the West and the Plains where it was difficult to enforce law and order because communities were scattered and often isolated. Drink was plentiful and cheap which also contributed to the lawlessness. Two pioneer women in Montana recorded their experiences:

> Murders, robberies and shooting are everyday occurences in daylight as well as at night. There are times when it really is unsafe to go through the main street, the bullets whizz around so. What do you think of a place where men openly walk around with shotguns waiting to shoot someone against whom they have a grudge, and no one attempts to prevent it?
>
> *Letter from 19th-century pioneers*

Drink was seen by many women as the greatest evil. It was seen as the cause of violence and the destruction of family life. Men who drank heavily put their women and children at risk, for they wasted their own wages, as well as any income their wives had, on alcohol. Families were left without sufficient money to buy food or pay the rent.

The demand for *prohibition* and *temperance* united large numbers of women in organisations such as the W.C.T.U. (Women's Christian Temperance Union). It was particularly strong in the 1850s in Kansas, but soon spread across the West and the Plains. Fanny Holsinger, a leading member of the

The results of a drunken brawl in the town of Hays, Kansas

Women and men attend a prohibition meeting in Kansas in 1878

Movement for Prohibition and Temperance, said of her campaign:

> Abolition! Prohibition! *Suffrage*! How we struggled for these issues in Kansas.
>
> *Fanny Holsinger, autobiography, in J. Stratton, Pioneer Women, 1981*

Once organised, the women were prepared, not only to preach the evils of drink, but also to take direct action against those who sold it. In 1858 a group of women in Kansas attacked a newly opened bar, brandishing a selection of axes and hatchets which they used to destroy every bottle and barrel they could find. During the 1870s, the temperance movement grew even bigger, and a group of women formed the National Women's Christian Union in 1874. Frances Willard became the leader and many women joined. By 1878 there were 26 local branches. A newspaper, *The Temperance Banner*, was published in the same year. Members worked hard, through debates, prayer meetings and classes for the young, to promote their cause. Women even held prayer meetings in bars, much to the annoyance of the drinkers.

In 1860 the W.C.T.U. had its first success when Kansas introduced prohibition. Once the sale of alcohol was banned, the illegal sale of drink commenced instead. Women such as Carry Nation were determined to stamp it out. In a brilliant campaign, Carry Nation publicly identified the offenders. As a result, Kansas City and Medicine Lodge became completely dry. Not content with this success, Carry Nation followed the drinkers to Kiowa some 20 miles away, where they had sought refuge. Having tracked them down, she destroyed the bars they drank in. As a result of her actions, the citizens of Kansas awarded Carry Nation with a medal inscribed 'To the bravest Woman in Kansas'. Later Carry Nation appeared in films and sold replicas of her famous hatchet. Unfortunately, the W.C.T.U. did not approve of this type of publicity, so Carry Nation was dismissed from the organisation.

In 1919 the W.C.T.U. was completely successful in its campaign. Under the 18th Amendment to the Constitution, the making, selling and purchasing of alcohol was prohibited. It was not until eleven years later, in 1933, that drink became legal once more.

Carry Nation being led away by the town marshall after delivering another stirring speech against the evils of drink, 1901

The struggle for equal rights

Women were involved in other campaigns too. A steady rise in the number of women factory-workers between 1850 and 1870 (making items such as clothes, cigars, umbrellas and shoes) and the number of women in other low-paid jobs encouraged trade unions to take women seriously. If wages were to increase and working conditions to improve, then women had to be unionised. In 1867, the cigar-makers' union became the first to allow women to join, followed by the printers' in 1869. Women also set up their own organisations to protect their interests and to fight for better wages and conditions. They funded the Working Women's Association whose membership was open to all women workers. Another women's group, The Protection Association, confined itself to

Women voting in Wyoming for the first time, 6 September 1870

helping women with welfare matters such as those relating to legal aid and to solving the problems of finding reputable employment.

Like the suffrage movement in England, which was gathering momentum in the 1860s, American women believed that the vote would give them the means with which to improve conditions further and gain greater equality. As early as 1848, Mrs Cady Stanton and Mrs Lucretia Mott had organised a conference to discuss women's rights. The meeting was a success, with 300 women in the audience. News of the meeting spread through newspapers, discussion groups and even the speeches of those who opposed it!

In 1859, three early feminists, Clarina Nichols, Mother Armstrong and Mary Tenney Gray, attended a meeting at which the constitution of the new state of Wyoming was being discussed. As observers, they could not participate but their presence helped to ensure that women were given the right to own their own property and to have equal custody rights over their children.

In 1863 a nationwide controversy broke out across the U.S.A. after the freeing of the black slaves in the South. Black men were now entitled to vote, at least in theory. Women saw this as their opportunity to push through their claim to suffrage.

However, it was the issue of race which split the suffrage movement. The proposed 15th Amendment to give black men the vote excluded women. Some suffrage supporters, such as Lucy Stone, were prepared to accept this, in exchange for the government's promise to support women's suffrage in the future. Others, like Elizabeth Cady Stanton and Susan Anthony, argued that if black men were given the vote, this would intensify sexual inequality. The issue of black women was ignored.

In 1869 Susan Anthony and Elizabeth Cady Stanton founded the National Woman Suffrage Association. Only women could join and the organisation was criticised for failing to address the issue of race. It did, however, concern itself with a variety of causes including divorce and the organisation of working women. In the following year, the American Woman Suffrage Association was founded, probably by Lucy Stone. This was a more conservative organisation which came to believe in white supremacy. Despite differences, both organisations actively campaigned for women's suffrage.

In 1869 Wyoming Territory became the first government in the world to grant women the vote, largely because women had played such an active and public role in its settlement. At the same time, a law was passed allowing women to own property and giving equal pay to male and female teachers. The women's names now appeared on the electoral role and they could be called up for jury service.

Elsewhere in the West, the battle continued. Canvassing, speeches and the publication of articles by women such as Abigail Duniway kept the suffrage movement alive.

In 1893 the women of Colorado were given the vote. Women in Idaho became *enfranchised* before the turn of the century. But for those in the remaining states of the U.S.A., the fight went on into the 20th century.

6 A clash of cultures

When white settlers moved West they took with them a stereotype of the Indian. An image of a barbarous savage was shown in paintings, preached in sermons and written about in newspapers, popular literature and magazines. Tales abounded of the cruel Indian who captured white women and forced them to marry Indian braves. For many women emigrants travelling West, the idea of meeting an Indian filled them with terror. One woman, for example, did not sleep at night nor undress for fear the Indians would capture her.

Women also found it very difficult to accept

White pioneers meet with Sitting Bull and his family in 1882. The photo shows Sitting Bull's ninth and last squaw, with three of her six children. The youngest one, on her back, is one year old, and the two twins, aged five, are sitting on either side of 'Little Bell'.

the culture of the Indians. They were even shocked to find that they did not speak English, or even French. Many were appalled to find that the adult Indians wore few clothes, whilst their children wore none. One typical pioneer, Sallie Maddock, thought that the Indians were disgusting and dirty looking.

Many white women settlers could not see that their way of living might seem quite ridiculous to the Indian. White women wore large uncomfortable hoops under their dresses and tight corsets to achieve the small waistline which was the height of fashion. It was even known for women to have their lower rib removed in an operation to ensure a tiny waist. People bathed infrequently but used huge quantities of toilet water to mask their smell.

A lack of appreciation of the Indian culture also led to misunderstandings. The Indians expected a gift when strangers travelled through their lands. This was part of their custom, but white travellers saw it as begging.

Coupled with this fear and disgust was a belief that white people had a moral responsibility to 'reform' the Indian. Nineteenth-century women were brought up to believe that they were protectors of Christian civilisation. It was their duty to civilise and convert the Indian to Christianity.

Sara Smith, a minister's wife, wrote:

> I long to be at my journey's end. I long to be telling the dying heathen the story of the cross. O, how happy I shall be in my labouring for the good of those dear Indians.
>
> *Sara Smith, a diary extract*

White settlers justified their claim to the land by viewing Indians as heathens and barbarians.

Despite the clash of cultures, a number of women changed their views about the Indians. Some recognised that tribes were very different from each other and began to treat Indians as individuals. Friendships were sometimes formed between Indians and white people. Some settlers traded with the Indians, and swopped ideas and remedies.

Before the arrival of the pioneers, the Indians lived all over North America

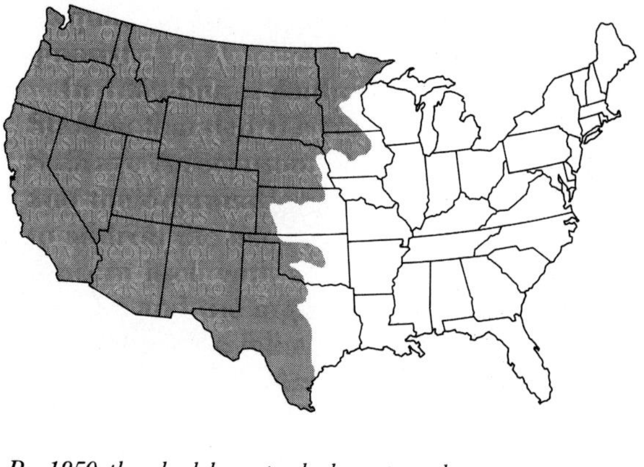

By 1850 they had been pushed westwards

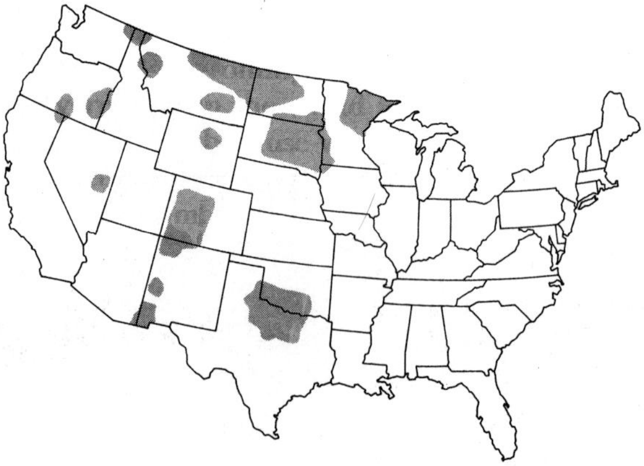

By 1875 much of the land had been forcefully taken away from the Indians and they were made to live on land specially set aside for them

Some white women were captured by the Indians and treated badly. Others were treated well. One woman, Ann Brewster Organ, was captured by the Sioux and married to a chief. She was later discovered and released but often wished she had never been found.

It was this change in attitude and a rejection of the stereotype that made some women believe that the cause of the violence on the Plains was as much the fault of the white settler as the Indian. Mary Hopping wrote how two traders had paid an Indian counterfeit money for a pair of moccasins. She angrily called the traders 'smarties' and felt that they had treated the Indians with contempt.

Elizabeth Custer told the story of the battle of Washita which took place in 1868. At this battle, her husband, General Custer, mounted a surprise attack on an Indian camp, killing 103 of the inhabitants. Only 11 of these were warriors. Elizabeth Custer wrote in her diary:

> It confused my sense of justice. Doubtless the white men were right but were the Indians entirely wrong? After all, these broad prairies had belonged to them.
>
> *Elizabeth Custer, diary*

Many male settlers appear to have clung to the stereotypical view of the Indian, as did many women. Some women, however, possibly due to their own changing position in white society, became far more sympathetic to the Indians.

It is more difficult to find out what the Indian women felt about the white settlers. There are few sources about this and what there are come mainly from the settlers, not the Indians. What we do know is that Indians had a very different perception of the white world. To them white Americans were strange creatures who did not respect the mother earth and who polluted the environment. Indians believed that the land, air and water belonged to everyone. It was not for sale. They were horrified by the settlers' desire to own land and fence it in. One Indian chief sums this up:

> How can you buy or sell the sky, the warmth of the land? The idea is strange to us. If we do not own the freshness of the air and the sparkle of the water, how can you buy them?
>
> Every part of this earth is sacred to my people. Every shining pine needle, every sandy shore, every mist in the dark woods, every clearing and humming insect, is holy in the memory and experience of my people. The sap which courses through the trees carries the memories of the red man.
>
> There is no quiet place in the white man's cities. No place to hear the unfurling of leaves in spring, or the rustle of insect's wings . . . And what is there to life if a man cannot hear the lonely cry of the whippoorwill or the arguments of the frogs around a pond at night? . . . The Indian prefers the soft sound of the wind darting over the face of a pond, and the smell of the wind itself, cleansed by a midday rain, or scented with the pinon pine . . .
>
> *Kangi Wiyaka, Crow Feather, oral account, late 19th century*

Today many Indians are fighting for their lost rights and challenging, through the American court system, what they consider to have been the theft of their land many years ago.

Questions

1 Look at the Introduction. What problems do historians face when trying to find out about the lives of women in the American West? Do you think the authors of this book have overcome these problems? Analyse the strengths and weaknesses of the sources used in this book.

2 Referring to chapter one: How significant was the role of women in the daily survival of the Indian tribes?

Many settlers did not sympathise with the Indian culture. As an Indian woman how would you reply to criticism of your way of life? You may include homes, work, food and general life-style in your answer.

3 Read all the evidence about what it was like to live in a sod house. Look at the pictures of homes. What does all this information tell you? Why do you think people lived in them?

4 Read the following extracts:

> A wagon load or two of people would soon invade the house of an evening. If the children were in bed it took but a few minutes to hustle them out, and then ensued an evening of frolic.
>
> *J. Stratton, Pioneer Women, 1981*

> There are few social events in the life of these prairie farmers to enliven the monotony of the long winter evenings; no singing schools, spelling schools, debating clubs, or church gatherings. Neighbourly calls are infrequent because of the long distances which separate farmhouses.
>
> *Atlantic Monthly Journal, 1893*

Read pages 26–7 about evidence of community spirit. What do the sources above tell us about the social life of pioneer women? Do all these sources say the same thing? In what way are these sources similar and in what ways are they different? Using your knowledge of homesteading women, say which of these sources you believe to be correct.

5 Using all the information from books you have read, write two letters from two different homesteaders showing your life on the Plains.

6 How important was women's contribution to the growth of towns? Do the photographs give a true picture of women?

7 Look again at chapter five. Draw a poster for the Temperance Society showing the evils of drink. Draw a poster arguing against prohibition. If these posters were to be used by historians in the future, what problems might arise? Why do you think women in the West and on the Plains gained the vote much earlier than women in the rest of the world?

8 Find out as much as you can about Indians today, now known as Native Americans, and their relationship with other American groups. Look in other books to find out what happened to Indians living in America.

Glossary

anthropologist someone who studies people and their origins

autobiography story of your own life

bee meeting for combined work and amusement

cholera an illness which causes diarrhoea and vomiting and can kill

Congress part of the American government

dysentry illness which causes diarrhoea and vomiting and can kill

emigrant someone who leaves one country to settle in another

enfranchise to give someone the vote

freight cargo

full to clean woven cloth

gall liquid which comes out of the liver

gelding a young male horse

huckleberry fruit from N. American shrub

husk dry outer covering of fruits or grain

immigrant someone who settles in a foreign land

itinerant travelling

lodge tipi or Indian tent

malaria a fever carried by mosquitoes

matrilineal descent through female line

moccasins deer-skin shoes worn by the Indians

okra a vegetable

parfleche rawhide that has been soaked in lye (strong alkaline solution) and water

patties small pies

pemmican dried, shredded meat pounded into a paste with fat and berries

Plains a wide open space which lies across the centre of North America

pleurisy a serious chest infection

pneumonia inflamed lungs

prohibition the name for the situation in which the selling and drinking of alcohol is forbidden by law

quilling weaving with feathers

quilting making a bed covering using cross lines of stitching

rawhide untanned leather

remuneration payment

scurvy a disease due to lack of fresh vegetables

sinew a piece of tough tissue which keeps the muscle and bone together

skillet a small metal cooking pan with a long handle

snakeberry a fruit

soapweed a plant which you can use as soap

sweated trade work in which people are forced to toil in poor conditions for low pay

suffrage the right to vote

tallow fat, grease

tan to convert a skin into leather

temperance restriction in production and drinking of alcohol

tipi Indian tent

travois a sort of sledge drawn by a horse or dog

turpentine a substance collected from fir trees and used in medicines

typhoid an infectious disease which produces red spots on the chest and can be fatal

zinc a white metal which can come in sheets and can be used in roofing

Further reading

J. Stratton, *Pioneer Women*, Simon & Schuster, 1981

J. Reiter, *The Women*, Time-Life, 1987

C. Lucetti with C. Olwell, *Women of the West*, Antelope Island Press, 1982

Frank B. Linderman, *Pretty Shield: Medicine Women of the Crows*, University of Nebraska Press, 1932, reissued in 1972

Acknowledgements

The author and publisher would like to thank the following for permission to reproduce text and illustrations:

Text Excerpts on pp. 7, 8, 9, 11–12 from *Pretty Shield* by Frank Linderman. Copyright 1932 by Frank Linderman. Reprinted by permission of Harper & Row, Publishers, Inc.; extract on p. 16 in Dorothy Sterling, *We Are Your Sisters: Black Women in the Nineteenth Century*, W.W. Norton & Co. Ltd. Copyright © 1984 by Dorothy Sterling; interviews on pp. 21, 22, 37, 38, 39, 41, 46 from *Pioneer Women.* Copyright © 1981 by Joanna L. Stratton. Reprinted by permission of Simon & Schuster, Inc. and International Creative Management, Inc.

Photos p. 7 courtesy of Museum of the American Indian, Heye Foundation, N.Y.; pp. 9, 14, 16, 21, 22 Peter Newark's Western Americana; p. 11 Picture from *People of the Sacred Mountain* by Father Peter John Powell. Copyright © 1982 by Father Peter John Powell. Reprinted by permission of Harper Collins Publishers Inc.; pp. 17, 32 reproduced from the collections of the Library of Congress; p. 20 Nebraska State Historical Society; pp. 24, 31, 37, 39, 40 (top and bottom), 41 The Kansas State Historical Society, Topeka; pp. 25, 26, 30 courtesy of Peter E. Palmquist; p. 27 State Historical Society of North Dakota; pp. 28, 42 Wyoming State Archives, Museums and Historical Department; p. 29 courtesy of the Buffalo Bill Historical Center, Cody, Wyoming; p. 33 (top and bottom right) from the Rose Collection in the Western History Collections, University of Oklahoma Library; p. 33 (bottom left) Arizona Historical Society, Tucson; p. 35 courtesy of the Alaska State Library, P.E. Larss Collection, PCA 41–54; p. 36 Keystone-Mast Collection, California Museum of Photography, University of California, Riverside; p. 38 Denver Public Library, Western History Department; p. 43 Montana Historical Society, Helena.

Cover illustration shows the Chrisman sisters, Nebraska, reproduced by kind permission of the Nebraska State Historical Society.

Maps by Jeff Edwards.

Illustrations on pp. 11, 23, 34 by Neil Sutton.

Every effort has been made to reach copyright holders; the publishers would be glad to hear from anyone whose rights they have unknowingly infringed.